SECRETS OF BUILDING MILLIONAIRE MINDSET

Simple Terms of Developing Habits, Ideas, Thinking and Maintaining a Long-lasting Successful Creation of Wealth

JENNER BROWN E.

Copyrights©2021 Jenner Brown E.

All Rights Reserved

INTRODUCTION

CHAPTER ONE

BOUNTY-THE MASTER PLAN

   The most effective method to pull in cash profoundly in 9 stages

CHAPTER TWO

INSTRUCTIONS TO SHOW CASH RAPIDLY IN 5 STAGES

  Here are a few ideas:

  Here are 20 amazing cash appearance insistences:

CHAPTER THREE

DIFFERENT WAYS TO DRAW IN CASH

INTRODUCTION

I recall when I was first investigating the law of fascination, I had done interminable examination on this. I had a strict foundation growing up. That implied a ton of odd stuff. So I'll concede, when I would look for "how to draw in cash profoundly," I was hoping to see stuff about customs and spells.

Fortunately, I know much better now, so I don't need to go through cash purchasing scented candles of specific tones. I can simply pursue a faster route!

What's your recurrence?

You can tell, in view of how you feel. Presently, ask yourself, truly, what is your opinion about cash? That should advise you precisely where you're vibrating at.

Cash HAS A Recurrence As well!

Truly. It does. On the off chance that you're constantly bankrupt, you know, you're not at a similar recurrence as cash. It's that straightforward. You can't be on a similar recurrence as cash, and not have any. Do you know somebody who gets a bonus of money, however after a brief time, they can't clarify how or why it's no more?

It is safe to say that you are this somebody? Does it happen way time and again? You should watch that you're on a similar recurrence as cash.

CHAPTER ONE

BOUNTY-THE MASTER PLAN

Get something – cash is just an image. It's a portrayal of riches, not abundance itself. You need to start to recognize the wealth surrounding you – the bounty that you are. Bounty is the capacity to would what you like to do when you need to do it.

In this way, it's not simply cash that can permit that. A companion could offer to get you passes to a show you've been needing to see. You could stagger on something important to sell.

It's not just about cash.

When you train yourself to perceive the bounty that is around you, at that point and really at that time would you be able to get appealing to a greater amount of wealth. Furthermore, that incorporates cash!

The most effective method to pull in cash profoundly in 9 stages

Stage 1: Notice What's Going Right

Truly, on the off chance that you invested some time to see the positive qualities in your day to day existence, appreciate it, enjoy it, at that point more will come. Regard for a subject brings more things like it. So focus on what's working out positively for you. Regardless of how little on the grounds that in all actuality it's not little by any stretch of the imagination.

Stage 2: Underestimate It

At the point when individuals talk about underestimating things, they will in general come at it from an exceptionally lackful perspective. It's not about not liking something. It's about what it implies in a real sense: Underestimate it! All the great stuff you want, all the cash you'd love to have, essentially accept that it is conceded to you! Simple.

Stage 3: Approve of Getting

Is it true that you are one of those individuals, who everytime they get a commendation, they react with a commendation as well? Or on the other hand something self-depreciative. Like, somebody praises your shirt. Do you say, "This old thing?" Stop. Kindly stop.

You're not helping yourself. Be available to accepting. For no obvious reason. You don't have to procure it. You don't have to put yourself down for having it simple. You don't have to attach yourself to a certain something.

Try not to box off roads for wealth and cash in your life by being respectful. Acknowledge! With a grin, and profound appreciation. You're awesome, and that's just the beginning. For no obvious reason.

Stage 4: Envision it

Truly, this ought to be number one. See, I'm continually going to say this, since I realize that it generally will be valid: creative mind is everything. I've had times where I entered an awful arrangement, or got some awful news. Promptly, I stop what I'm doing, unwind, and afterward picture a scene where what I needed occurred. I can't reveal to you how regularly I've gotten twofold or triple what others would say I "lost." How? Just by envisioning unique.

Realize that the world is yours, and it will form itself as indicated by what you envision it. Envision the well off, rich adaptation of yourself. At that point...

Stage 5: Become it.

How? There's no interaction to this, not actually. Simply be the individual with all the cash you want. What might you think about your bills? About putting resources into land? When you go to the store, would you purchase the peanut butter discounted, or the one you like? The rich variant of you would go for what they need. This doesn't mean you should start to spend it like insane when you don't have. It's OK on the off chance that you don't have the chilly, hard money right. Simply know since it's not there, doesn't mean it's not there.

Stage 6: Get settled

We've discussed how accepting your new persona (the rich you) can feel awkward or abnormal before all else. Like getting into another suit. (Alright not the best model, but rather you get what I mean.) You should simply work on being in the condition of a rich individual.

Before all else, you may see yourself talking, thinking, feeling, or acting in manners that don't coordinate to Rich You. Try not to whip yourself. It really is great that you took note. Just shift once again into the rich perspective and being.

Stage 7: Envision

Indeed, this was referenced previously. I notice it once more, since it's significant. Envision being praised on your prosperity. Envision taking your loved ones out for a rich supper at a costly café – and paying! Envision tipping the server twice or threefold the bill, for kicks. Envision, envision, envision.

Stage 8: KNOW It Is Finished

At the point when you've made yourself OK with being rich, by envisioning yourself around there, there isn't anything left to do, yet to realize it is finished. So when another bill comes in, there's no compelling reason to freeze. You believe it is dealt with. You do all that can be expected at that time about it.

Yet, suppose you get the bill, and you feel that smidgen of tension eating at you. At that point follow this subsequent stage.

Stage 9: Overhaul

Modification is a stunning device for transforming you. Trust me, I know. I modify all the awful stuff that occurred for the duration of the day. At that point around evening time, Not long before bed, I make it a highlight go over my day and change the awful to great. I likewise change on the spot as well, when I get news I don't care for, or have an encounter I could do without.

I simply slip into a casual, neglectful space, and afterward supplant what occurred with the image I like. At that point I emerge from it and approach my day. Innumerable supernatural occurrences have happened to this! It's OK in case you're kicked out of the condition of feeling like you're rich. However, when you notice, just get back in, and afterward amend that.

On the off chance that you saw a bill and terrified, return, see the bill once more. See yourself being careless about it. Far and away superior, see yourself making the installment there and afterward, a grin all over! The best part about modification, isn't just would you be able to amend the awful stuff and make it great – yet you can change the great and improve it!

Correction is an incredible asset. Use it however much you like, and have a great time!

What's in your ledger? Try not to like it? Update it! What's your FICO rating? What sort of house do you live in? Whatever it is you can consider, can generally be better.

What is cash sign?

To show cash is to bring cash into your real life utilizing your musings, convictions and sentiments. This is conceivable since everything is energy, including cash.

CHAPTER TWO

INSTRUCTIONS TO SHOW CASH RAPIDLY IN 5 STAGES

Before we get into the means, I need you to realize that you are completely fit for showing. You don't should be a mystic or have a third or fourth eye open. You are showing constantly!

Your musings, emotions, and convictions get occasions into your life and have brought about how your life looks like at the present time. By changing your opinion, you can transform you.

Presently it's an ideal opportunity to quit showing obligation and monetary inconveniences, and show cash and a bountiful life all things being equal.

1: Say farewell to your restricted convictions:

The vast majority got modified with restricted convictions effectively in adolescence by our folks and society. We're told: It's smarter to be content than rich, Cash is the base of all abhorrent, Cash can't accepting satisfaction.

A large portion of us actually convey these restricted convictions, intentionally or unknowingly. You won't ever have the option to turn into a cash magnet in the event that you don't relinquish these convictions. You need you change your inside before you can change your outside. Record every one of your convictions, musings and sentiments about cash.

I suggest ruminating for a couple of moments prior to beginning, so you are more in touch. Tune in to an entrancing for eliminating cash obstructs on YouTube consistently before you rest, Contemplate and envision your ledger brimming with cash. Record each restricting conviction on a piece of paper and consume them individually. Feel how they are leaving your body

Make a rundown of confirmations, for example, "I'm a cash magnet", "I draw in cash, simple and easily" and so on Recite it so anyone can hear each day, and FEEL the bounty you have in your life.

Write in an appreciation diary each day what you feel thankful that HAVE in your life. It very well may be something as little as having a rooftop over your head, or how honored you are that you can manage the cost of the espresso you're tasting on each day

2: Counterfeit it until' you make it

I took in this progression in the law of fascination book of scriptures The Mystery. Act as though you're now rich.

How might a rich individual respond? How might they dress? How might they act?

What's more, no, I'm not saying you should proceed to purchase a Gucci purse or a personal luxury plane, it's about the little things. For what reason would it be advisable for you to go through the difficulty of doing this? As I said before, everything is energy and vibration, so when you FEEL rich you are in the bounty vibration. At that point it's more uncertain for those negative musings to spring up and make bounty blocks.

So what are some little things you can do to feel rich and bountiful without wearing out your wallet?

Here are a few ideas:

Begin giving modest quantities to a cause you feel energetic about

Give some food or coins to a hobo and wish them a lovely day

Begin dressing tasteful and rich, similar to you have cash. Discard your loose shirts with openings and smudges and get some new, new garments. No requirement for costly fashioner garments here, simply take a gander at how they dress and get a less expensive adaptation at H&M, Hole or another spending attire shop

Compose a check to your future self and put it some place you can see it consistently, as Jim Carrey!

3: Raise your vibrations

Your vibration can be considered as your energy field, and the fiery responses going on in your body. The higher it is, the more lined up with your actual higher self you are, and the simpler it is to show anything. Counting cash and bounty. Attempt to avoid things that bring down your vibration, similar to the dread based news, thrillers and individuals who channel your energy.

Pick a couple of these vibration-raising hacks and carry out into your life as day by day or week by week propensities:

Think for in any event 10 minutes day by day. Ideally toward the beginning of the day, as it at that point keeps you in a high energy state for the remainder of the day

Ground yourself – walk shoeless external day by day

Remember more ALIVE nourishment for your eating regimen – like vegetables and natural products, ideally crude and natural. The more toward plant-based you can go the better

Exercise – pick something you appreciate, regardless of whether that is tennis, moving, climbing, and running and so on, Scrub down, Do yoga, Be in nature

4: Make an enlivened move towards your objective

There appear to be two camps with regards to cash making – in the business local area it's tied in with trying sincerely and hustle. The harder you work, the better the outcomes, they say.

In the otherworldly local area, it's tied in with plunking down and picturing that check until it comes.

There should be an equilibrium. We've effectively covered own to change your inside. Presently it's an ideal opportunity to make a move. "The Universe can't help a vehicle move that stops. You need to as of now be making a move towards your fantasies." So in the event that you need to turn into an affluent writer, begin composing, each day.

In the event that you need to turn into an affluent YouTuber, make recordings, consistently. In case you're battling to remain gainful, there are numerous approaches to give your mind a lift.

I take this nootropic yet I've likewise heard beneficial things about this science-based music administration.

Follow your instinct on which heading to go in, at that point make a move towards it. At that point you are adjusting to what you need to show. The Universe sees that you are not kidding about it and can help you.

5: Acquire the adoration recurrence

The most elevated vibration of everything is the adoration recurrence. The most impressive approach to pull in cash quick is by being in the vibration of adoration when you consider cash.

What are a few different ways you can do this?

Imagine burning through cash on your loved ones and how cheerful they look

Make a dream board, an actual one or on the web, for example, on Pinterest. Fill it with rousing pictures of what you need to purchase with the cash you will draw in. Take a gander at it consistently and be grateful that you will actually want to pull in this

Focus each time you have a negative idea and supplant it with affection. For instance, when you get a bill, rather than feeling down, shift into adoration and appreciation. Be appreciative you are helping someone's business, and that you can stand to cover bills and have a rooftop over your head.

At the point when you're working, contemplate appreciating what you're doing, being of administration and be glad about how you are being of help to other individuals, instead of zeroing in on bringing in cash.

Which mantra is incredible for cash?

Like I said in the stage 1, rehashing mantras or confirmations consistently as a component of your routine can be an extremely amazing approach to draw in plenitude into your life.

What you can do is select 10 of these enabling cash proclamations, print them out and put on your mirror. Rehash them each day gradually, and truly FEEL how they are valid.

It's vital that you require some investment to feel this, as they will not have a lot of impact on the off chance that you have questions.

Here are 20 amazing cash appearance insistences:

-I'm available to get abundance from numerous points of view.

-I decide to carry on with a rich and full life.

-As I bring in cash, I'm prepared to give and serve liberally.

-I'm open and open to all the abundance life offers me.

-I will respect my fantasies and advise myself that I merit achievement and joy.

-I'm deserving of getting more cash.

-Cash comes to me in expected and unforeseen manners.

-My activities make steady thriving.

-I'm open and responsive to all the abundance life offers me.

-Bringing in cash is something positive that serves me, my family, and my local area.

-Cash streams unreservedly to me.

-My business is developing, growing, and flourishing.

-Cash grows my life's chances and encounters.

-I'm deserving of all the lavishness I want.

-The more I give, the more I get. The more I get, the more I give.

-Cash awards me openings and new encounters. Cash upgrades my life.

-I'm a cash magnet.

-Each dollar I spend and give returns to me increased.

-I use cash to better my daily routine and the experiences of others.

-I'm the expert of my abundance.

What is the best tone to pull in cash?

A notable Feng Shui secret is that red is perhaps the best tone to draw in cash. Red is the shade of solidarity and force – simply consider the inclination you get when you see individuals strolling down an honorary pathway or a ladies wearing a radiant red dress.

The Chinese accept that this is the shade of bounty and abundance, and is accordingly ordinarily found in Chinese organizations.

Another cash pulling in shading is, of course, gold.

Some great methods of getting a greater amount of the gold vibration in your life is to enhance your home for certain brilliant things or by wearing gold adornments.

Drawing in Cash Is Simpler than You Might suspect draw in cash. In the event that you need to realize how to draw in cash into your life, you have gone to the opportune spot.

Most importantly, pulling in cash begins in your mind. You should have an uplifting outlook and a decent cash mentality. Besides, you need to make a genuine evaluation of your present cash state. Also, create of vision of how pulling in cash into your life affects your future. At long last, make the correct moves to get more cash-flow. Also, go through your cash shrewdly.

CHAPTER THREE

DIFFERENT WAYS TO DRAW IN CASH

Presently, how about we go through every one of these cash certifications in more noteworthy detail. At that point you also will know the mystery of how to draw in cash and riches. Regardless of whether you are beginning your cash venture without any preparation. Revelation: At no expense to you, I may get commissions for buys made through joins in this post.

1. To Pull in Cash, Have an Inspirational perspective

Have an inspirational perspective. Take a gander at the brilliant side of things. Try not to harp on the negative. Practice positive self-talk with regards to cash.

By being positive you will pull in better individuals to connect with. What's more, those better individuals will help you on your excursion to a bounty of cash.

Practice Positive Self-Talk, I just referenced positive self-talk. What precisely is that?

At the point when adverse occasions or slip-ups occur, positive self-talk tries to deliver beneficial things once again from the negative. To assist you with doing, go further, or simply continue to push ahead. The act of positive self-talk is a cycle that permits you to find darkened idealism. Additionally, the expectation, and the delight in some random circumstance.

At last, definitely, have faith in yourself. What's more, what you are attempting to achieve with cash. Pulling in cash through the law of fascination requires this. On the off chance that you don't accept, who will?

2. Make a Beneficial Cash Outlook

Your cash outlook is the manner by which you consider cash. Any you need to center the uplifting outlook we just talked about towards cash. You should accept that you can dominate your cash. That you can get more cash-flow. Also, set aside a greater amount of the cash you make. Consider abundance and cash in a decent light. Once in a while individuals with cash are vilified by government officials and the media.

As a general rule, the vast majority that are fruitful in drawing in cash presently are persevering, upstanding individuals. There isn't anything amiss with having cash. Or then again attempting to draw in more cash than you as of now have. In light of my encounters, stressing has no worth. Regularly, cash issues make pressure in our lives that lead us to stress. Stress and stress can separate us. It can make medical problems. It can freeze us up and keep us from our mission to pull in cash at home or work.

Along these lines, it's imperative to oversee pressure viably. I know everything excessively well. I'm a lovely high-stress individual. Furthermore, have had periods in my day to day existence where stress basically injured me. Understand that the vast majority of the things we stress over never occur. Whenever you are worried about cash, consider your cash outlook.

Most importantly, move your contemplations on to something more certain. Since whatever you are stressed over likely will not occur. Moreover, make a move to lighten your concern. Is there is something you can would about the issue that is on your care? Assuming this is the case, definitely, do it?

In the event that you need to realize how to draw in cash profoundly, stress and stress should be controlled. Doing so will draw out your internal strength and resolve. Alright at this point. That closes our first key takeaway territory. The most effective method to draw in cash utilizing mind power. Keep in mind, everything begins between your ears.

So now, we are prepared to take a gander at the second large space of this subject. That is, understanding your present status of issues with regards to drawing in cash quick and as time goes on as well.

4. Acknowledge the obvious issues and Make a Fair Appraisal about Your Cash Status individual accounting.

Get your monetary realities together. What is your total assets? How much cash do you spend and where do you spend it. A free online device like Individual Capital is an incredible asset to evaluate your present monetary state. Furthermore, deal with your cash adequately.

Do you have speculations? At that point, what are they and are they the correct ventures to accomplish your cash objectives. Thus, invest some energy getting comfortable with your accounts. To draw in cash at home, make a region where you can zero in on your cash.

A home office is an ideal choice. Yet, it very well may be anyplace you want. However long you can get to your cash related data.

5. To Draw in Cash Spotlight on Wealth and Be Thankful draw in cash immediately.

Presently you have a superior comprehension of your present cash state. Along these lines, make a bounty mentality about what you have. Try not to stress over what you don't have. At the point when I get down about something, I consider this expression. "I'm feeling down in light of the fact that I had no shoes until, upon the road, I met a man who had no feet."

End of conversation? Be appreciative for what you have. What's more, don't harp on what you don't have. A plenitude mindset will benefit you. Continuously recollect that numerous individuals have short of what you.

6. Offer What You Have

Remember to offer in return or give to noble cause if that is a significant thing to you. Giving is one of numerous amazing abundance insistences. I'm not enthusiastic about parting with our cash. In any event not yet. Be that as it may, a few group depend on it with regards to drawing in cash.

Maybe giving cash to noble cause is simply unrealistic given your present money related situation. I comprehend. Yet, sharing doesn't need to be just about giving cash. It can as straightforward as this. Put a grin all over and share it with the world. Carry out something beneficial for a neighbor or companion.

As my mom used to say, "You receive back twice as much consequently as you give." And my mom was in every case right. At any rate that is the thing that she advised me! Alright. That covers the second key territory in our mission to pull in cash. That is surveying your present status.

As a matter of first importance, comprehend your present cash circumstance. Besides, see that circumstance with a bounty attitude. At last, be liberal with what you have. Then, on to our third key region on the most proficient method to collect your vibration to draw in cash. It is deciding your future state.

7. Make an Investigation of Abundance to Pull in Cash pull in cash, riches, and achievement.

What is riches? What amount of cash do you require? How individuals that have been effective in pulling in cash approach doing as such? These are for the most part vital inquiries. There are a large group of assets on cash, abundance, and abundance expanding nearby here at Profits Differentiate.

I invite you to look at any of these articles about abundance building. Yet, I will call attention to one so you don't get overpowered. Why study riches? All things considered, how might you understand what accomplishment with cash resembles in the event that you don't? You might be confused about riches and how to assemble it.

Furthermore, that drives us to our subsequent stage during the time spent how to pull in cash. It is deciding your future state.

8. You Should Envision Cash to Pull in Cash draw in cash utilizing mind power.

When you go on an outing, would you have an objective in care? Obviously, you do. Not many of us get in our vehicle or get onto a plane without a reasonable thought of where we are going. Turning into an achievement in drawing in cash is the same.

Pull in cash into your life by having your objective at the top of the priority list. Prepare to stun the world and accept in the event that you can imagine it. At that point you can accomplish it. That is the reason our past advance was to find out about riches. To make your vision you should comprehend abundance building.

A Speedy Recap on Our Status of Pulling in Cash

We are currently prepared for our fourth and last key territory to pull in cash. Since a large portion of what we have examined up to this point has been applied. Also, key.

Most importantly, we set up a positive cash outlook. Moreover, I had you survey your present status of cash issues. At last, you have made an investigation of abundance. Also, figured out what your objective of pulling in cash resembles.

However, presently, we are prepared for more strategic advances. What do I mean by that? Indeed, the embodiment of pulling in more cash boils down to 2 essential zones. Above all else, getting more cash. Moreover, going through less of the cash we have. Furnished with your present status. Also, future cash objectives. You are presently prepared for these more solid activities for a wealth of wealth.

9. To Draw in Cash Put Yourself "Out There"

We as a whole, somewhat, dread disappointment and dismissal. In any case, you can't protect yourself from those things. Disappointment and dismissal accompany facing determined challenges. Try not to fear disappointment. Embrace it. I like this adage, "when one entryway shuts, another will open". I believe it's actual valid.

Whatever it is you accomplish professionally, don't stow away from it. Or then again, as I like to say, "Put yourself out there". Furthermore, put yourself out there in a positive light. Search for the following chance to get more cash-flow. Regardless of whether it's functioning harder at what you do. Setting yourself in a place for a raise. Or on the other hand getting another, better paying position.

The objective is to augment your procuring potential. In any event, making a little side hustle cash may help.

10. Think regarding Adding Worth, Not Time abundance confirmations.

Trying sincerely and investing the effort is significant. Try not to misunderstand me here.

In any case, you would prefer not to exchange time for dollars when endeavoring to draw in cash. You need to consider increasing the value of whatever it is you accomplish professionally. Ask yourself how you can help your organization, your client, or your manager succeed. That is the way you convey esteem. You can even do this for cash from a commonplace the lowest pay permitted by law work. Here is a model.

At the point when I was in secondary school and school I worked at a café and bread kitchen situated on 15 sections of land of property. It was a lowest pay permitted by law work, in addition to tips when I tended to tables.

Gradually, however unquestionably I continued assuming on greater liability. I did arranging on the grounds. Tidied up tables, looked out for tables, served drinks, and set up for enormous gatherings and wedding gatherings. At last, when the kitchen was short-staffed, I assisted with kitchen arrangement work, washing dishes, and tidy up. So, I made myself priceless to the activity. My chief, the proprietor, consistently had work for me to do.

Why? Since I generally searched for ways and territories I could add esteem. What's more, make the foundation run better. Make it a superior spot. I wasn't hesitant to "put myself out there". Adding esteem and doing the correct things the correct way is the thing that pays enormous cash over the long haul. Consider how you can do this in your circumstance. You are just restricted by your innovativeness and the disposition you take.

11. Focus on Persistent Personal growth law of fascination.

Putting resources into persistent improvement is quite often a decent spot for your time and cash. Be it books, classes, certificates, or hands on preparing.

Simply ensure your self-speculation is lined up with your lucrative spaces of core interest. Recall this colloquialism… "be preferable today over you were yesterday and preferred tomorrow over you were today". Then, we need to discuss the going through side of drawing in cash into your life.

12. Go through In Arrangement with Your Qualities

Choose what you esteem throughout everyday life. Is it travel, a delightful home, flavorful food, live amusement? I don't have a clue what it is really going after. Furthermore, what you worth may change over the long haul. It has for me. Bringing in cash and spending it on what you can.

13. Minimize your belongings to only what you need and use. Be minimal with your finances by streamlining and simplifying them. Buy what you need and want. But don't consume just because others are doing so. It is contradictory in some ways, but I like to say "minimize your finances to maximize your money".

14. Reward yourself how to attract money

Identify and celebrate the little successes along the way. I'm not so good at this one. I set a goal and work hard to accomplish it. But when I do, I tend to move on to the next thing. Even if you are like me in this regard, from time to time sit back and reflect on and enjoy your accomplishments.

Last but not least, we have point number 15 on how to attract money. It may the most important.

15. A Fast Formula for Attracting Money: Take Action

Nothing will happen unless you make it happen. So take action.

Start working on these 15 tips about how to attract money now. So you will have money in the future. They are the things that separate the wealthy from the poor, in my opinion.

www.ingramcontent.com/pod-product-compliance
Lightning Source LLC
Chambersburg PA
CBHW070907220526
45466CB00005B/2163